Dear Love...

Love,

Freez

Dear Love... Love, Freez
ISBN 978-0-615-28959-5

Freez 4 Life Entertainment
4422 Falcon Meadow Dr
Katy, Texas 77449

Published by:
Freez 4 Life Entertainment
4422 Falcon Meadow Dr
Katy, Texas 77449

Table of Contents...

Preface...

In no way is this a plug for my macking and sexual prowess (although, I do the damn thing), but I have been blessed to have been with, what I believe to be, some of the most beautiful women that God has ever created. Beautiful black women of all shapes, shades and styles. Older and younger, tall and short, intelligent and sometimes not so much. For many of these ladies, I have nothing but good to say. For those others, the ones brothers worldwide have experienced, we'll just save those for another time. Enjoy!

(Names and locations have been changed to protect the identities of both the innocent and the guilty!)

To Love…

I walk this path looking for love,
Yet the coast is always clear
Never to have loved at all,
This is my truest fear

Although, I've been in love before,
Your assumptions are completely wrong
I've been in love with myths & ideas,
Sappy movies & slow love songs

I want a love so true it hurts,
Too stimulating for me to sleep
A love so strong it helps me reach
My mental, physical and spiritual peaks

I dream of an everlasting love,
A love that sees me through
In this life I live my dream,
My dream of loving you

Introduction...

Life is a crazy thing sometimes. Boy meets girl. Boy and girl fall in love. Somebody messes it up. The love never dies, but hearts and trust remain broken. If you are the cause, you'll do anything to make it right. Unfortunately, things can never really go back to how they were. Sometimes, it gets better, sometimes it gets worse.

So this is my love letter/apology to love, to all the ladies that I have loved and lost, and to anyone that is lost in love. If you have it, hold onto it. Cherish it. The only thing more beautiful is the love that God has for you.

This is a story of love. This is a story of loving love. This is a story of losing love. This is a story of learning love. This is my story.

I have always loved love. I have always longed for love and have always loved to be in love. Ever since I was a little shortie, love has been one of, if not the, most important thing to me. There just isn't anything else really worth the effort, other than the love of the Lord, which is supreme over all. During the times that most people experience and realize true love, they are engrossed in that atmosphere. There is usually little to no time to worry about meaningless items like bills, grievances with others, and in some instances, things that aren't so meaningless, such as eating.

Besides, who wants to worry about such matters as these when you're in love? If the bill is late, don't worry, they will still accept payment. If someone is upset with you, they will get over it... and soon be angry again. If they don't get over it, do you really want to be bothered with them? Last, but not least, who needs food when you're being sustained and nurtured by the nourishment of love? (I don't know about you, but I'm getting my grub on.)

By no means should you be under the wrong impression. This is not a book about what people should be willing to sacrifice in the name of love. Instead, it is my love letter to love. It is my apology to love. These are the stories of all the women that I have loved and lost. Hopefully, for the women and men that are lost in love, this will be an inspiration; something that will encourage you to be not only seekers and givers of love, but lovers of love as well.

Introduction to the Love of My Life...

(Whomever she may be)

Shhh, be quiet, I've got a secret to tell
But I won't tell no one else, I hope you'll be keeping it well
Look here... I've been sitting back, checking your style
Just for a while, and I'm already in love with your smile
So can I get to know your name & get to know your mathematics,
Get to know your mannerisms and your slightest habits?
Girl, I've got to have it, so I won't leave without it
I can't live without it, I live for truth & in you I've found it
A diamond in the rough, a pearl from imperfection
A sheep in wolf's clothing, but still I'll give you my protection
Respect, love and affection, and admiration too
For all the trials and tribulations you've made it through
I could be made for you, and you could be made for me
Tomorrow is a brand new day, we can just wait and see
'Cause I don't want to rush it, that may not be for us
There could be something totally different you see for us
You don't know me from Adam, you can't tell me from Steve
But I'm the coldest man on the planet, just call me Freez

And I'm so pleased to meet you, girl, I've got dreams to know you
And anything you need to know about me is my dream to show you
I'm a man of action, I've just got a way with words
You can get away with murder, mesmerizing me with those curves
Let's shop for his and hers, be friends or say goodbye
Either way, I'll be straight, I just can't leave saying, "What if I...?"

My Angel...

All I really need right now
Is someone who'd be true to me
So, usually, I'd think about you and me
And how times used to be
'Cause you would be there for me always
To help me grow and learn
I've always known I could come to you
When I had nowhere else to turn
So, I'm writing this to you,
In hopes to show my love
To show my thanks to my lovely angel,
Whom God sent from above
I thank you, Tierra, and I apologize
For all the times I've made you mad
I must admit, I hang my head
For all the times I've made you sad
There's nothing I could do for you
In order to make it right
All I can do is for myself
And straighten out my life
Although, it's not too bad right now, I'm still lost and confused

Trying to fight this fight alone,
I end up battered and bruised
I won't ask for your help this time,
I've done that too much before
This time I'll have to learn to seek my refuge in the Lord.

I don't remember the exact date anymore, but the memory is still very vivid in my mind. It was late spring of '94, and I was only fifteen years old. We were all in Sunday School; Cam, Ciara, myself and the rest of the crew were in class, when in walked two very cute girls. Originally, I thought Yvonne was the one closer to my age. She was tall, with long hair, and had a very fair complexion. Tierra, the pecan-toned younger sister appeared to be younger than myself. I will never forget the simultaneous and instant feelings of attraction and disappointment the moment I saw her. Don't get me wrong, Tierra was, and still is, a very beautiful young lady. It's just, at the time, I refused to talk to any girl younger than myself. I had always grown up around older folks and didn't relate very well to most people my own age, let alone younger.

Both girls were forced to stand and introduce themselves to the rest of the class. Shyly, they spoke.

"Hi. My name is Yvonne, but people call me Von. I am a senior at Cypress Falls and I'm eighteen years old."

"My name is Tierra. I'm a sophomore at Cy-Falls and I'm 16." Eureka! "She's older than I am, and she looks just like Ashley Banks (my second tv wife, from *The Fresh Prince of Bel-Air*)." I loved Tierra instantly and have ever since.

We began to get to know each other over the phone, but because we were both so young, neither one of us had a car, or a driver's license for that matter; we were at the mercy of church functions and gatherings whenever we wanted to see each other. I really don't recall whether or not we decided to "go together" at the time, but in my head, she was already my wife. We didn't do much together, but whenever we were together, it was obvious to all who saw us that she was my lady.

I loved spending time with Tierra. She *still* has a certain innocence about her that is undeniable. Now, I'm not one for much talking when there is nothing to talk about unless we're playing the dozens, and that wasn't Tierra's thing. So her shy, quiet demeanor was perfect for me. We would just spend time together and enjoy each other's company. Sometimes, she'd be doing her thing and I would be doing mine. We were high school sweethearts from the end of our sophomore year until I came home for good from the Navy. One of the many things that I still regret to this day, is not taking her to neither her nor my senior prom.

Graduation came and three days later, I was on a plane to Great Lakes, Illinois, headed for United States Navy boot camp. While in boot camp, I learned to meditate somewhat to the image of Tierra's face in my mind, taking my mind off of the recruit division commander and the homesick feeling in the pit of my stomach. I started remembering everything that we had done together, everywhere we'd gone. Suddenly, and without warning, I was struck by a revelation; I had never actually seen Tierra do anything I could recognize as sin, whatsoever.

I understand that sin is much more than what we do, that it is our very nature. Realizing that I had never actually seen her sin was very surprising, given the type of girls that I usually dealt with. I loved, and love Tierra, but I could not and did not see her sin. Not then. Not now. That intimidated me immensely and still does to some point. All you have to do is look at me to see the results of just one of my sins. Keep reading and you'll find evidence of even more. Nonetheless, from the moment I realized that fact, Tierra became my angel.

It's a funny thing to love someone that you feel less and less comfortable around. It wasn't that she made me uncomfortable. I did that all on my own. It was my sins, my skeletons, my secrets that kept me from developing the type of bond with Tierra that I dreamt of having. Back then, to me, love was nothing more than a feeling; it was what you felt. It didn't involve putting forth any effort; it just happened or it didn't. It was what it was. I didn't know then that love was a verb, a call to action, a call to cherish, a call to adore. I have always felt love for Tierra, but I am filthily guilty of loving her very weakly. It was at that time that the feeling of love had some major competition... from the feeling of being unworthy.

One of the things that I have learned during my brief time on earth is that when a man fears that he is in danger of losing something or someone that he dearly cherishes, he will do one of two things:

He will either make the necessary changes to
maintain what he desires
OR
He will make no changes for fear of
making the wrong ones.

Unfortunately, I chose the latter, but the love was always real. Nevertheless, I never stepped up to the plate to be the man that I felt she deserved because I felt that I was not that man. My own sins paralyzed me from being the man I wanted to be, not only for her, but for myself as well. Instead of giving her all I had, I took away some of the things that I had already given her. Because I felt that way, I prevented myself from doing the things for her that I wanted to do all along. I didn't call much, even when I wanted to. We didn't talk much, even though I wished we had. We didn't do much, even though I felt that we should, but to this day, I still love her.

I didn't want Tierra to keep falling blindly in love with

me and then one day open her eyes and see what I had believed all along, that I didn't deserve her and she deserved much better than me. I wanted her acceptance and approval (which I already had) so much that I was afraid to receive it properly. So, I pushed her away. I knew that if I had let myself receive her love and acceptance at its fullest, I would have to be *that* man.

Over the next year and a half, I tried to take steps and gradually become the man that I wanted to be for her. I would take her out and call her for a while, but sooner or later, the calls, visits and dates would cease. I wanted to tell her so much how I wanted to love her for the rest of my life, about how I wanted our future daughter to be her spitting image. Instead, I kept it hidden in my heart, tired of being a man of only lip service.

Until one day, I did it. I made up my mind to love the one woman who had always been there for me whenever I needed her. Hers was the shoulder I cried on. Her ear was the one I told of my feeling of being unworthy. Her letters kept me sane while I was away. How could I ever have had the nerve to not love her the way that she so rightfully deserved? How dare I not give her the full attention and affection that I knew she craved?

It was time.

I couldn't believe that she would actually have me back again, or even be open to the idea. I was so happy and determined to make sure that I stayed on top of making her number one in my life that I left a drunken message on my brother's voice mail, asking that he would stay on me to make sure that I did exactly what I said I would do; treat her like a queen. That's when the unthinkable happened.

The night I made my new resolution to be the man that Tierra deserved, wanted and needed, we were at a mutual friend's birthday party. We talked and I made my decision, then and there, to love her. After I'd left the party, I experienced an incident that would change the rest of my life from that moment forward. I fell asleep behind the wheel, wrecking my car, causing explosions that would lead to the amputations of both of my legs.

While going through the pain of rehabilitation and readjusting, I fell so deeply into depression that life seemed useless. I wasn't seeing life with the eyes of a sane man. At that time, I had given up on living and focused on killing myself without committing suicide. I decided that I was going to smoke weed and pop ecstacy until God saw that I was dead serious about dying and allow me to come home.

I had left Tierra once for the Navy and hated myself for years because of that. The reason is that when I did come home we were pretty much finished as a couple. Even though, the love was still mutual. When I came back, she told me that she no longer wanted to be in a relationship. So, like a man trying to save face, I said the same. I tried to woo her back, but that old feeling of not being good enough scared me into mediocrity and guarded feelings.

After the accident happened, when I found out that she had actually gotten physically ill over my trauma, I wanted to die then more than ever. So, when I decided to focus on living a dying life, I knew that I didn't want to take her down with me. That's when I came up with the "Pam scheme."

Tierra was faithful and loyal, almost to a fault, if there is such a thing, so I knew I had to do something drastic in order to get her to see that it was time for her to move on with her life. As previously stated, my life was in an intentional downward spiral. My brother knew how I was feeling and what I was going through, but he did not know what I was planning. He couldn't, not if I was going to be able to pull it off.

Pam and I were just friends and she and Tierra were best friends. Pam also had somewhat of a crush on my brother, Cam. Funnily, Pam and I spoke more than she did with Cam and more than I did with Tierra. I told my brother that I was going to try to sleep with Pam, and just as expected, he told me that it would ruin everything I had with Tierra, which I already knew.

I invited Pam over to the house and told her to make sure that she came alone. Pam's cute and everything, don't get me wrong, but she couldn't hold a candle to Tierra. To me, she was always "Big-Head Pam," and there was never more to our relationship than being friends.

When she came over, we went back to my room. I laid on the bed and she sat next to it in my wheelchair. Honestly, it looked like she had done herself up a little bit, but that was none of my concern. We had a little small talk and then I did it. I broke it down to her as lame as I could, like a weak business proposition. I asked her straight out, straight up. No feeling. No desire. Just a question. Even though I didn't expect her to go forward with me, I was surprised by the fact that she said that she thought that was the reason I invited her over. That caught me off guard until I remembered how I had emphasized that she come alone. She agreed to allow me to tell Tierra, and I honestly expected for her to grant that. I guess I shouldn't have been shocked by the fact that she decided to protect her own back, and I don't blame her.

The very next day, unexpectedly, Tierra and Pam showed up to my apartment with just about everything that I had ever given to Tierra. It hurt to have that happen, but for the life of me, I don't know why I didn't expect it. Tierra, Pam and Cam all went into his room and they told him about "what happened." Even though some of the details that Cam relayed to me were more than embellished, it was of no consequence. I refused to tell "my side." I accepted the blame, offered no excuses and, put forth no defense.

Not long afterward, I realized how grand of a mistake my plan was and I have regretted it ever since. Not in a romantic sense, but out of compassion. I still loved Tierra, but I knew that I was not the man for her. I still loved and love Tierra, and wanted to kick it with her from time to time. Only thing was, we had always kicked it like boyfriend and girlfriend, and I didn't want to go there. I rarely talk to her now and I never see her, but she will always remain close to my heart.

My Vixen...

Front seat, middle lane of a three lane street
She brings heat from the passenger seat
A hazardous feat
Jazzy sweet to my fantasy freak
Asking me can I hack it
Is she challenging me?

Hazardous passion in the middle of traffic
Where is the plastic?
Snatch it open, attach it
Pull over, turn on the hazards

Jazzy chic doing nasty shit
And I'm attracted
Like a moth to a flame insanely drawn to its tragic end
Gladly falling in like a tailspin
From the tail end
Roll the L and dwell in the spell we fell in
Keep inhalin'

After Tierra and I decided to split when I came home from the Navy, I tried to hide my pain in PWA: p***y, weed and alcohol. Around that time, I met Cheyenne, a beautiful woman with an ear to ear smile and a bubbly personality that you just could not be down around. We met at a club in downtown Houston over the Christmas break of '98. I had just returned home from the Navy, and Tierra and I had just broken up for good. Cheyenne was home from Texas A&M University.

I noticed her in the club, but I also noticed how many other brothers were noticing her as well. I chose to let the situation be, but she'd noticed me also and wanted to dance. I didn't want her to see how attracted to her I was, so, I played it like it was just another song and just another dance with an anonymous girl. I was glad to see that her interest was just as high as mine. She would not allow me to leave without taking her number... And you better believe I took it.

Come to find out, Cheyenne was home from school not only for the Christmas break, but also to have a cosmetic breast reduction. I visited her at her home after her surgery, and even though she was doped up with no make-up, she was still beautiful. I loved to be around her. While she was on bed-rest, we spent that time getting to know each other. Most of the time we spent talking, and what we talked mostly about was who was going to be responsible for making sure that we didn't rip each other's clothes off the moment she completely healed from her surgery. The sexual tension between us was so strong that it became the focus of all of our conversations.

Even though I was fresh out of the longest relationship

of my life, I did want something serious with Cheyenne. However, she was home only temporarily from school and I didn't want to be a victim, yet again, of another wilted, long distance relationship. But what we had, I didn't want to lose. I wanted to have my cake and eat it too. Even though she was only a few hours away, I made it perfectly clear to her that I was not going to involve myself with another long distance relationship, no matter how badly I wanted to. Boy did I want to. Nonetheless, we carried on with our relationship as if we were never to separate. However, we were very unsuccessful at maintaining a sex-free relationship.

We decided to go to one of her friend's New Year's Eve party and got just a little too tipsy. While everyone was chilling and conversing in the front room, we decided to slip away to the back bathroom and have a little intimate time alone (classy, I know). It turned out to be one of the most memorable nights of my life. Despite the lack of my sexual climax, this was one of the best sexual encounters that I have ever had in my life. Time appeared to fly by until, about an hour later, we received several anxious knocks at the door impatiently informing us that our time was up.

The next day, I messed up and lost her trust in a very unexpected way. I knew that I should have called her the next morning, but I was falling too deep, too fast. I let the day go by without a call and she definitely let me hear about it when we finally did speak. She let me know that she had been hurt by my actions, or inactions rather, and that she didn't appreciate that at all. From that point forward, our conversations became a lot shorter and much more formal. When we were together, I spent more time trying to find the right things to say instead of just talking to her. I was looking for a way to get back into her good graces, looking for a way to keep the lines of communication open for when she went back to College

Station because I really didn't want to lose her... Too late.

Cheyenne wasn't going for it. She decided that enough had been enough and that it was time to return to Austin with a clean and fresh beginning. I sparingly kept in contact over the next few months because I knew that she would be back for the summer. When she arrived that summer, I tried to mend the relationship and she gave an honest attempt, however, there was still much resentment.

I'd applied for enrollment at Morehouse in their Pre-Freshman Summer Program. I didn't tell Cheyenne about it because I didn't plan on getting accepted, nor did I have the funds to pay for it if I were. God acted on my behalf, as only He could, and not only was I accepted, but accepted without having to pay the full fee for the summer program. It was all last minute, so I wasn't able to inform Cheyenne with any future notice of my departure. I did tell her immediately before I left, and unfortunately, she was under the impression that I had known the whole time. She left me with a few choice words, "You ain't shit. You ain't gon' be shit, and your kids ain't gon' be shit."

Over the years, I have tried to reconnect with her. However unsuccessful I have been in that effort, I wish her nothing but joy and success.

My Dawg...

You've got me sittin' mesmerized
By the sight of your eyes
In a trance
And it's your glance that I can't stand to deny

Take a chance
Approach your stance and your devilish smile
Your mellow-ish style
Goes good with a fellow this wild

You ready to ride?
Come on, baby, slide in
Your sly grin makes me wanna do
How they did at drive-ins

Once Cheyenne and I had gone our separate ways, I met Melyssa, My Dawg. To this day, she is the only woman that I have ever been with that was truly both a lover and a friend. Not to take anything away from any of the other girls I had been with, but Melyssa was and is "da homie." There was just something about Melyssa that allowed me to be the same me that I am around my boys. I didn't always have to have good manners, or speak proper English, or speak much at all for that matter.

I met her during Christmas break of 1999 at Texas Southern University. I was helping Henry move his girlfriend's furniture from her dorm room back to her mother's house. Melyssa was also moving out with the assistance of a couple of friends. She was wearing a maroon track suit, so, obviously I thought that she was on the TSU track team. Our eyes locked instantly and my eyes followed her all the way to her car. After I had taken Kori's belongings to her car, I strolled over to Melyssa's and did what I do.

This time, I was the one visiting home from school in Atlanta. I was debating on whether or not I would return to Morehouse College because I knew that I didn't have enough funds to pay for the spring semester. My pastor issued me a check for what I owed for the previous semester, which would have allowed me to go ahead and enroll for the spring. Even with that, I still wasn't sure that Morehouse was the place for me.

Anyway, since I was home and I knew I had to go back to Atlanta, at least to pick up the rest of my things, I made sure that I enjoyed every minute I was home. Melyssa and I started to spend a lot of time together because we clicked automatically. With Melyssa, it was different from any other relationship I had ever previously been in. She allowed me to be me completely. I could talk to her using the same tones and words that I used when speaking with my boys, and I could speak on the same subjects. I'd heard a lot of girls say that I should feel comfortable talking to them about anything, but rarely did they want to hear the "anythings" that came out of my mouth. Melyssa was the only girl that I have encountered who I can honestly say held true to that statement, though she never made it. She didn't trip, at least not with me around, regarding me telling her about some of the other girls on her campus that I'd been with before and during our time together.

We were never actually in a committed relationship. Although I did ask to be, she thought it would be best that we get to know each other a little better. Instead of taking her advice with the appropriate concern that she held, I took it as a slap in the face.

"Wait? How dare you deny me? Don't you know how many of your girls want to be with me? I know you see this six foot four frame and you have the nerve to tell me to wait? "

Pride is a bastard-maker and a love-killer, and I had more than my fair share. At that point, even though I did not inform her, it was pretty much over in my mind as far as a commitment was concerned. I still liked Melyssa and enjoyed being with her, but the sting of what I took as rejection prevented me from ever opening up fully. We still kicked it and grew closer and closer, but because of the wall I put up, it just wasn't the same. On my part, it became much more physical and much more carnal than actually trying to connect on any type of spiritual or emotional level. I was no longer interested in a relationship, only relations. As much as I liked Melyssa, I liked my own self-image a lot more.

I'm not sure if she noticed, or how much she noticed the change in my thought process. But if she noticed at all, I couldn't tell. Everything continued on as before, except for the change in my focus. We continued to spend a lot of time together and continued getting to know each other. One day, we got a little closer than I liked, resulting in a tacky passion mark high upon my long neck, too high for any collar to cover. Now, I have nothing against passion marks as long as they are properly placed, but please, please don't put one on me for the entire world to see.

I know that I can be an unfair brother at times, but I'm not so unfair that I would leave her alone over this one incident. This one incident, however, was just a little too close to the "rejections" I had experienced previously. I decided to let her know how I felt about misplaced passion marks and that if it ever happened again, it would be the end of us.

I doubt that she believed me because not long afterwards, she put me to the test. We were in her dorm room, just chilling. We were on the bed, watching tv or listening to the radio or something like that. Now, Melyssa is a five-foot-nothing little woman who loved to play-fight and wrestle. We started playing and after a while, I led her to believe that she had pinned me. I'm not one for much play-fighting with women because I don't like the idea of getting used to putting my hands on a woman in any inappropriate manner.

As I lay on my back, she straddled me and started trying to put a passion mark on my neck. Initially, it felt good, so I really didn't pay any attention until I noticed that she was doing more than just necking. I pulled away from her and it turned into a game. She tried to give a hickey while I blocked. It went on for a couple of minutes and I reminded her about what I had said at the time of the first hickey. She said she remembered.

"Well, if you remember, do what you do."

Dammit, she did it. I laid there without trying to stop her and she went at it like a brand new Hoover vacuum cleaner. Never before and not since has a woman sucked my neck quite like that. My neck looked diseased. I couldn't believe it and I couldn't take my eyes off of the reflection in the mirror. I hadn't seen a bruise like that on my own body since my high school football days. All that went through my mind was, "I can't believe that she did it. She actually did it. I told her what would happen and she did it anyway. Now I *have* to keep my word, otherwise she would be doing it all the time." So, keep my word I did.

I didn't even want to, but I had to. Laughing the entire time to keep from showing my true emotions, I picked up my things and got ready to go. She walked me down to my car and all that ran through my mind was how badly I didn't want to do what I felt I had to do. I leaned in for the usual goodnight kiss. Instead of kissing her on her lips as I usually did, I averted to her cheek as she closed her eyes, and strolled silently back to my car.

To her credit, she did call and apologize, but I felt like, "What good is an apology when she did it on purpose? If I do take her back, what's to stop it from happening again?" I just couldn't bring myself to give her the forgiveness that she wanted.... That I wanted... That we wanted.

My Heart...

Your eyes pierce my soul from across the room.
Your lips hypnotize me as I watch you speak.
I smell your eternal, internal sweetness with each exhale.
I get lost in the rise and fall of your chest with each breath.
I long to lay my head on your soft, firm stomach.
Although pride won't let me show it,
I get jealous watching your right hand caress your left.
Your belly button beckons me, longing to be teased.
Can I taste your soul?
I dream of wearing your thighs draped over my shoulders,
Tasting your sweet champagne,
Pulling you closer as you pull away.
Does it feel good?
It tastes good.
It's too hot to be cold, so I know why you're shivering.
Would there be a problem
With me licking honey from the small of your back?
Or whipped cream from your...?
Would you like that?
Can I pour chocolate on your delicate feet,
Just to make the chocolate a little sweeter?

Would you mind if I made love to you until...?
Soft and tender, at first,
Slowly increasing intensity,
As the orgasms build up inside you,
'til you feel your stomach caving in?
Don't quit on me now.
The night's just begun and the fun ain't over.
When we first met,
You had me paralyzed by the movement of your mouth.
Now, you biting your lip and your quivering jaw
Give me all the gratification I need.
Are you in a trance?
Open eyes not seeing.
Clear ears not hearing.
Too sensitive to be touched,
Yet feeling everything.
Feel me again.

The same year I met Melyssa, I met Yvette, my heart. I fell in love with Yvette after our third conversation. We met in a club parking lot while everyone was leaving. She and her cousin were spying on her friend's man and I was there with my family for my brother-in-law's birthday party. Yvette was yelling down the street at some truck peeling off, so, in a flirting manner, I told her to keep it down, walked over to her car, and again, did what I do.

I waited a few days before calling because Valentine's day was right around the corner and I was trying to be fly. When we talked, I felt like she was trying to play me sideways. She wouldn't open up to me so I didn't open up to her. On the third conversation, it happened. I don't know what "it" was, but whatever "it" was, "it" made me see Yvette in a whole new light. The more we talked, the more I knew that one day soon, she would be mine. Unfortunately, Yvette was adamant about us being just friends. First date, no kiss, didn't try. Second date, no kiss, tried but denied. She was serious.

The third date came and we did the same thing that we did for the first two, chilled at the crib. If I'm not mistaken, we were watching the movie *Life* with Eddie Murphy and Martin Lawrence. D'Angelo's *Untitled (How Does It Feel?)* started to play on the radio in the background. All of a sudden, we were in a lip-lock and embrace for the next fifteen to twenty minutes. It was totally unexpected for me, but I'll be damned if it wasn't wanted.

After the kiss, I knew I had her. It was just a matter of time and I let her know that. A couple of weeks went by when one day, I was at home watching television and talking to her on the phone. I reiterated to her that I felt we should, and would, be together. Her position remained constant, so I didn't push it. We hung up the phones and she called back an hour or so later, emphasizing the thought that we should remain "just friends." I could tell that she was no longer trying to convince me, but herself. About three or four hours later, she called me and asked, "What are we?"

From the conversations that we'd had just a few hours earlier, I knew that she couldn't be asking the question for herself. I thought about blowing up the spot on her, but not knowing who she may have had on three-way, I said that we were only friends.

"See Mama, I told you we were just friends."

"See Mama? " I thought. She wouldn't need to convince Mama unless Mama thought otherwise... And Mama knows. With all this evidence, I would have had to be a dead, blind man in order not to see that she was fighting what she was feeling. Over the next few weeks, we continued to play the same game. Friends. More than friends. Friends. More than friends.

One night, we were over her house watching tv from the sofa. We began to get a little frisky and she laid a kiss on me that honestly and literally took my breath away, leaving my lips tingling with enjoyment. I had never been kissed like that up to that point and never since. To this day, it remains the best kiss of my life.

Up to that point, Yvette was under the impression that I was only around because I wanted to have sex with her. I admit that it was partially my fault. My game is strong and I know it. Yvette and I were talking loud, saying nothing one day. Just talking a lot of shit really. She was talking noise about the different things that past men had done in order to win her affection, and I was talking about my game. I made the mistake of saying that I could have had her in less than two weeks if that was my only aim. Either I didn't emphasize the contingency of my bold declaration or she didn't pay any attention to the contingency because, all she heard was, "I could've had you in two weeks."

Despite her reservations, we began to get very passionate that night. We moved from the sofa to the floor and clothes started to fly. Initially, I was excited that she finally decided to open up this much to me. After a few moments of kissing and caressing, I remembered what she thought my sole intention was. I wanted her to realize that I was there for much more than sex. I wanted her to realize that I wanted to be with her and only her, and that love-making would be the icing on the cake. I wouldn't have tripped if she decided that we needed to abstain until marriage.

In an effort to get her to see my true intentions, I got her hot and bothered to the point that I knew that she would not be able to say no, got up off of the floor and, without a word, sat back down on the couch, leaving her wondering what in the world was going on. She gathered her clothes and joined me back on the couch. We sat there in silence for the rest of the evening and didn't mention it the rest of the time that we were together. Unfortunately, she never caught the significance of what I had done.

Obvious at this juncture, we decided to take the relationship to the next level, commitment. I was already committed to her and her to me, but we had never actually made it official. Late one Friday night, leading into the wee ours of Saturday morning, we talked about how things should be, what our level of commitment would be to each other. After we arrived at an agreement, at around two in the morning, we were both full of love and wanted desperately to see each other, so we decided to go out when I got off of work the following evening.

Well, I got off work about five that evening, came home, called Yvette and got ready to go. While we were talking, she informed me that she was ten minutes away and that she would be on her way as soon as she dropped her kids off at her cousin's. A few hours later, my brothers Cam and Henry came home, and were getting ready for Henry's last night of freedom with the boys before going to boot camp. While I talked with them as they got ready to leave, I got more and more frustrated waiting on Yvette. Ten minutes turned into two hours. Two turned into four. By this time, I figured I had been stood up and decided to go out with my brothers instead. Maybe a half hour passed by after I had made my decision when Yvette knocked on the door. She showed up with her kids and her cousin and was still not ready to go out, but she looked better than I had ever seen before. I was upset because I felt I had already been stood up and that was compounded by the fact that she showed up at my place unannounced, a definite no-no, and still unprepared.

I let her know that we weren't going to be going out together, that I was going out with my brothers instead. Well, she didn't like that very much and said that I was always putting my brothers over her. She was still upset from the weekend before when I didn't cancel plans with my brothers to spend time with her. That weekend was supposed to be Henry's last free weekend before he was given a one week extension. I had been drinking a little bit by that point, but I was not belligerent or disrespectful. I told her that because she stood me up, I would be going out with my brothers and that she and I could discuss whatever needed to be discussed in the morning.

I know that she continued to brood over it after she left because she called me from her cell phone, in my apartment parking lot and when she arrived home, trying to talk me out of going with my brothers. I maintained my position because I didn't feel that I was doing anything wrong because she was the one who stood me up. She was upset to the point that she told me never to call her again. By that time, the malt liquor began to take effect (I'm an Old English man myself) and all I said was, "Cool," hung up the phone, and went out with my brothers.

I knew what she said and I knew what I was saying and doing, but I didn't expect that to be the end of our relationship. The fact that we couldn't maintain our agreed upon commitment for even twenty-four hours was totally ridiculous to me. Pride got in my way, once again, and instead of calling Yvette the next day, I chose to let three or four days pass before I called. We were cordial and spoke civilly, but we were both hurt and neither of us wanted to give any ground.

We never resolved any of the issues that we'd had and we didn't really discuss what happened from our own perspectives until we were both in long term relationships. Funny thing though, we both agreed that we would rather be with each other than our respective partners, but what happened before left us both gun shy.

My Sorrow...

How do you make someone love you,
Who doesn't want to stay?
How do you leave someone behind,
Who just won't go away?

I ask myself the first and realize
I have to let you go
You ask yourself the latter and decide
You have to let me know

Without you I have nothing
So I have everything to gain
I want to share it all with you
Instead, you throw it all away

When I really like a woman, I know it in my heart very soon, sooner than the average person. It doesn't take me much time to figure out whether or not I would like to seriously pursue a relationship with a woman. With Tierra, I knew the first day and it couldn't have been more than five in-depth conversations with the rest of the women. On rare occasions, I would inform the object of my affections and attention of my feelings, even if I may have thought it was a little premature. Hope was one of those rare occasions.

We met in our initial training class at Verizon Wireless. Usually, in a new environment like a new job or class, if I don't already know the people, I play it cool. I try to weed out the fake ones by allowing them to hang themselves. I watch and wait for them to open up to each other and see who is doing the backstabbing.

Hope walked into the training class looking jazzy as hell. But, like I do, I played it cool, not wanting her to see that I was so attracted to her.

Over the next few weeks, the entire class was getting to know each other, everyone except myself. My aloof disposition earned me the reputation of a "pretty-boy thug" or a "pretty-boy trying to be a thug." I didn't pay it any attention. I was keeping my eye on Hope and on everyone else, still in recon mode. I determined that there were a few people I could be cool with, and others, not so much. Hope was very friendly, at least with me. Occasionally, we would go to lunch together or take our breaks together, but nothing big.

One day while we were on the phones, she wrote her

name on my hand. I took it as though she was staking her claim and told her that she forgot something. With no other word from either of us, she came back and wrote her phone number under her name.

It was cool talking with Hope because she allowed me to be myself, but also made sure that I maintained a certain level of respect. It didn't take long, maybe a couple of weeks, before I told her how I felt about her and that I wanted to be with her. She agreed and we pressed forward, together.

Not much time passed when I began to notice that she didn't seem to be as into me as I was into her, so I began to pressure her. I knew that she wasn't ready for a relationship, but you do not tell a black woman what she is, and what she is not, ready for. I had made that mistake only once before. When she realized that she wasn't ready, she came to me and told me and it was no problem because I had already known.

Afterwards, when we decided to go back to how things were, it did actually return to how it was before. Most people say, "Let's go back," but things are never quite the same. Not in this case. Not with Hope. We continued to kick it and spend time together and soon enough, we decided to try it again. Same thing happened.

As far I'm concerned, I'm not too big on the "make-up-to-break-up" relationships, but damn if we didn't do it over and over again. When I had my car accident, Hope was also at the party, but we weren't together at the time. During my stay in the hospital, the only people at the hospital more than Hope, were the doctors and the nurses, and I'd bet that she beat out some of them.

Hope was very supportive. She allowed me space to be depressed and sad and to wonder what was going on in my life. But, she would not allow me to wallow in self-pity and depression. Over this time, I developed a strong dependency, almost to the point of addiction, on Hope, but she had to get back to her life.

I was in the first hospital for about a month and a half and Hope's constant visits were what kept me sane. Looking forward to seeing her actually kept me from doing something to harm myself. Life was pointless. I used to be an athlete (football, basketball, swimming, boxing, etc.,) and I was tall, bright and handsome. All of that had just been taken away from me. I clung for dear life to the one thing that seemed to remain constant. Over time, however, Hope returned to her life and couldn't be there for me as before.

Although a lot of my attachment to Hope had to do with the fact that she spent so much time with me in the hospital, I did have valid feelings for her. Before the accident, I was able to see the kind of person that Hope was and that was what I liked. I liked the way that she carried and presented herself, like a lady. I liked that she was intelligent and ambitious, spoiled as she was. All of this was reinforced by her visits. Despite the countless times that Hope had stood me up, despite the numerous long periods of time that I didn't hear from her at all, despite the fact that I loved her through all of that, she was and is under the impression that my feelings for her were and are based solely on the hospital experience.

We still tried several times to see if we could make it work, but I wanted to love Hope, and not have to prove that I did. Nevertheless, we still remain good friends to this day.

Conclusion...

From all of these different relationships, I am able to find many positives, some points of light to which I can continue to strive towards. I've learned various things about myself, about women (though I fear I will never understand them), and also the differences between men and women. Women feel loved when they feel understood and cherished, men when they feel appreciated and trusted. Most problems arise in relationships because women give men the kind of love that they wish to receive and men do the same. No one is being loved the way that they feel they should be and we wonder why no one seems to be happy.

From my relationship with Tierra, I learned to appreciate, to the fullest, each second that I spend with the woman that I am in love with and I also learned how to love. Love is more than a feeling. It's an action. It's a continual action. Even more than an action, it is a moment-by-moment decision. I decided to run from and push Tierra away instead of loving her and showing her the love in my heart. I learned that even if I don't feel worthy of such love, I should still continue to do whatever is necessary to maintain that love if I really cherish the relationship.

In my relationship with Cheyenne, I learned that there are some things that just happen, things that are unavoidable, therefore, no one is at fault. My dealings with both Melyssa and Yvette taught me forgiveness and that love for myself is important, but that too much self-love doesn't leave much room for me to love anyone else, or allow them to love me, for that matter. After God has forgiven me for so much, how could I have had the nerve to not forgive Melyssa for something as fleeting as a hickey? I also learned much about pride. Check your pride at the door. Pride is a bastard-maker and a love-killer and there is no room for this destructive element in any relationship looking to mature.

With Hope, I learned that love is shown, not proved. I had already known for quite some time that my disfigurement due to my accident played a major role in Hope not wanting to pursue anything with me any further. Her saying that I was only in love with her because of the time she spent with me at the hospital was just an excuse, I believe, to spare my feelings.

Taking into consideration all that I have been through for the sake of love, and with all the pain that I blamed on love, I can truly say that there is nothing else that I am more interested in pursuing. There is nothing on earth more valuable than love. Nothing more noble. Nothing more delicate. Nothing more intimate. Nothing more precious. Nothing more deserving of my attention, affection and dedication. All of the heartache, all of the let-downs, all of the hurt I've felt, I would gladly experience a second and third time to experience true love just once.

If you have love, hold onto it and don't let it go. Make that special someone in your life feel that they are your life. Cherish each moment together. Tomorrow is not promised to anyone, so live and love for this day as if it were your last.

Love Always,

Freez

One Last Plea...

(To all the women I have loved and lost and to the ones that are lost in love.)

I wish you would've wanted to love me
I wish you would've wanted to hug me
I wish you would've wanted to slug me
At least you would've been right there
Or at least it would've shown you care
Or, at least I would've known I could get in your head
Maybe then I wouldn't act like a kid
But look, that's my past
I've been working on changing my scenes
I gotta get you back as my queen
I'm trying to let you know your every wish is my dream
If it'll get you back on my team, I'll do anything
I'm sorry for the times I was trippin'
I'm sorry for the times I ain't listen
I should have heard you from the beginning
Plus I'm sorry for the times that you missed me
I should have loved you more when you kissed me
And I shouldn't have needed this to convince me
But I've grown up

So please understand, now you can trust me
And it ain't just about how you touch me
It's more than that
'Cuz I'm willin' to push that aside
If you said we needed to, to survive
Until we see eye to eye
Or until the day I make you my bride
Until when down that aisle you stride
Until then, I'm yours
I hope you can see past your resentment
Believe, this is my truest commitment
I can't lose you again
You helped to raise a man from a child
Now I just pray my love can help make you smile
Even if just for a while
But even if it's just for a while
And then we come upon the end of our mile
The love was real

What is Love?

(interview transcript)

Conducted by: Franchell Jones

Franchell Jones: So I can have some clarity, and we can have our little intro-view, tell me about your cd.

Freez.Eternal: Basically, it's -- it's the poetry that goes along with the book, and the book, you know, it's a bunch of short stories about relationships I've been in, what I've learned and things like that. How I handled those situations and some poetry to go along with it, so I decided to put the poetry on CD and make it a package thing.

FJ: So, when did you write the book? I didn't know there was a book.

Freez: Actually, the book's been in the works for a few years. I wrote it a while back for the most part, set it down and forgot all about it. Went through some personal things and ended up coming across it during a move and proceeded with it.

FJ: Interesting. So you were inspired to do a CD based off of going through some things and then finding the book? Or you always planned to do a cd with the book?

Freez: Actually, the CD was basically, I won't say last minute, but it just came along with the book, once I actually got back to the book and started working on it again.

FJ: Ok, cool. Well, moving on. Tell me about yourself. Like, your stats... Age?

Freez: 31.

FJ: Height?

Freez: I was 6'4".

FJ: Weight?

Freez: Around 235.

FJ: Single, married, other?

Freez: Single.

FJ: Kids?

Freez: Nah.

FJ: No kids. Girlfriend?

Freez: Nope.

FJ: No girlfriend. Looking for a girlfriend?

Freez: (laughs) Nah, I wouldn't say exactly "looking," but not running either?

FJ: Interesting. So, do you have a goal? A relationship goal for yourself?

Freez: Yeah, I wanna get married and do the whole little family thing.

FJ: How old are you?

Freez: 31.

FJ: 31. This whole getting married, have a family thing, plan on doing that in your 30's? Seems like a good time for most.

Freez: Yeah, that would be good... umm.. 30's would be cool. I almost did it a couple years ago, but...

FJ: But?

Freez: Things happen.

FJ: Such as?

Freez: Life.

FJ: Interesting. Now, you know, we're having a interview here. So that means when I ask a question, "things happen" is not gonna work.

Freez: Nah, I almost got married a couple years back. Things didn't work out. She went her way; I went mine.

FJ: Interesting. Is she married now?

Freez: Not that I know of.

FJ: So do you think you guys could, I don't know, meet up someday, re-hash, and maybe it'll be all good? Like, the whole 'time away' thing?

Freez: I think we might be able to be cool, but, I think, in order for me to make that wanna happen again, there are some changes that I would have to see in her; the same thing for her. In order for her to wanna make that happen again, there are some changes she would have to see in me. I don't think either one of us are willing to make those changes, so...

FJ: Interesting. So let's say you were out and about. You say you're not looking, but you come across a female that intrigues you, what would that female look like?

Freez: I don't know. It depends on what she looks like.

FJ: I mean, people have preferences.

Freez: Yeah, we got preferences, but...

FJ: You're not firm in your preferences?

Freez: Not physically, nah. I mean, I like tall, short, thin, thick, light, dark...

FJ: Interesting.

Freez: Physical can vary.

FJ: Right, right, right. What about other than physical? What would she look like? For example, as far as education, career, etc. What kind of person would she be?

Freez: I don't really define people a lot by stuff like physical or factual type of information, but as long as she's smart enough to hold an intelligent conversation... Gotta be a Christian, that's number one.

FJ: Now when you say, "Christian," what exactly do you mean? Do you mean, she believes in God? She goes to church? Sometimes on Sunday, but maybe not, if she's got something going on the night before? Devout-like?

Freez: I mean, for me...

FJ: There's varied Christians out there.

Freez: I'm not gonna judge nobody and their walk with Christ. That's between them and the Lord. But she gotta be walking with Him. That's pretty much that. She gotta believe in Him. You know what I'm sayin'? And see some evidence of that in her life, I think.

FJ: Now, do you have an age preference?

Freez: For the most part, I've always talked to females that were older than me, so I wouldn't even know a number to go down to.

FJ: So, let's say you met a 21-year old...

Freez: (Laughs)

FJ: What?... No?

Freez: I mean, she'd have to be really mature, period. Not just for her age, but at 21, that's -- I like women, I don't like little girls.

FJ: Interesting... Hair?

Freez: What about it?

FJ: A lot of men have issues with hair, or they have preferences about hair. Do you have those?

Freez: As long as it looks good, I ain't really trippin'. I prefer natural. Not necessarily natural, but you know, not un-be-weave-able. But even if you're gonna do the weave all the time, just make sure it looks good. You know what I'm sayin'? But I prefer just the... you know, it's yours, you woke up with it, grew it yourself. All that.

FJ: Right, right, right.

Freez: Greased it, all that.

FJ: Oooh. Okay, greased it. So then, having said that, are we restricting ourselves to one race or could this lady be any ethnicity?

Freez: Hmm... I have a feeling that she could be of any ethnicity, but I usually feel more connected with my sistahs. So, I'd be a little bit surprised if it went a different race. But, you know, I'm not gonna limit myself on love just cuz the female I'm having those feelings for isn't Black or African American or Negro or whatever we are these days.

FJ: Any of those titles... Gotcha... How many times have you been in love? Or have you been in love?

Freez: Yeah, I would definitely say that. I would say that my most recent time would be my new definition of being in love, if not even something more than that.

FJ: Do you believe in love at first sight?

Freez: (Sighs) I believe in infatuation at first sight. I think that can definitely happen, but love? I mean, love is not just a feeling. You know what I'm sayin'? It's an action. Just because you see somebody and you get a certain feeling, that don't mean you love them. That feeling can lead you to doing things, you know, that don't display love by your actions, so... Yeah, I'll say infatuation at first sight.

FJ: All right. So could you give me an example, you know, like, the top three of love actions?

Freez: Top three love actions?

FJ: Yeah. Like, you say you love someone, how can they tell?

Freez: I think that's between two individuals to know between themselves. Because, I could do one thing in one relationship that female A would look at and be like, "Oh, he really loves me," and it may be something that female B totally overlooks altogether. Usually, I think it's some of the small things... when you've actually gotten to know who the person is, when you're doing something "for my girlfriend," instead of "for a girlfriend of mine." When you're doing something specifically for that person, and they know that you probably wouldn't have done otherwise or for anybody else. Those little-bitty things, those little things.

FJ: Do you have -- Well, first of all, let's say, you've been around a female and obviously you've taking a liking to her. Is there a process by which you go to, I don't wanna say -- Do you have a courtship process?

Freez: I don't know. I was getting schooled on courtship and dating and the whole nine and what the difference is a couple months ago.

FJ: Really? What did you take away from that?

Freez: Not much. I still don't really know what that difference is. I don't know. I mean, like...

FJ: Do you do a lot of dating?

Freez: No.

FJ: No dating.

Freez: I mean, I date, occasionally, but I don't do a lot of it. I know some people that's...

FJ: Always going out?

Freez: Yeah... That's not me... How do I go about -- Like, if I'm interested in a woman? Period, point blank, I mean, I let her know straight off top. I don't beat around the bush. I don't have no lines or nothing like that. I've never really been good that way. I just try to be honest, you know... "I would like to take you out. I think you're attractive. What's happening?"

FJ: Okay. So, what would be your idea of a good date or something you would like to do with a person that you have interest in?

Freez: A good date... Like, what's being done? It really wouldn't matter. To me, a good date really depends on the chemistry with a person, you know, between the two people. If we're not really laughing or smiling, then that's obviously not really a good time, but...

FJ: Okay. Well let me rephrase the question... Okay, a location or an activity...

Freez: A location or an activity...

FJ: That you think would aid in the date going well. For example, movie dates are for people who don't wanna talk. Cuz basically, what you're doing is, "Okay. let's go out. Let's go see a movie..."

Freez: Sit down and shut up for the next two hours.

FJ: Basically. For two hours, you're not talking to anybody and you don't have to look at them. So, that's a good date for somebody that you don't really particularly care to be around, or you're not sure...

Freez: I don't know. Some of my best dates have been movie dates.

FJ: After the movie?

Freez: Like, during the movie and the whole nine. I -- You know, I got a sense of humor or whatever. I like to joke and play around...

FJ: So you talk through the movie?

Freez: Oh yes ma'am. Fa sho. I ain't loud, but...

FJ: You said that you are not actively looking, but have you ever thought of, I don't know... doing one of the... what is it... speed dating, online dating, anything of that nature?

Freez: I got a couple pages up on the different social networks. I have met some females off of there. But, first and foremost, I'd rather meet a female in person, face to face. That's how I've always been. I like to deal with people face to face. I used to work on the phones and I know people can be one way over the phone and a totally different person, you know, in person. They take on that alter-ego over the phone or whatever, so I like to deal with people face to face.

FJ: Have you ever researched any of your potentials online?

Freez: Any potentials?

FJ: Yeah, like, let's say you met a girl and you thought that she was nice, but you weren't quite sure about her background. So you went online to JIMS to check and see if she had a record or some court cases you might wanna know about. You went to check and see if she's on America's Most Wanted...

Freez: (Laughs) I've never done anything like that. If I even feel like I gotta do that, it's time to go a different route altogether anyway. (Laughs)

FJ: What?

Freez: What'd you say? What was the name of the website?

FJ: JIMS.

Freez: (Laughs)

FJ: You've never been on there?

Freez: Never even heard of it.

FJ: You know what? That's all right. That's something for another day.

Freez: I think that's more of a female thing.

FJ: Yeah, probably so. There's a lot going on out there. I think guys should do it too though. Never know what you're coming up with. So, no online searches, but you have postings and listings online. That's good... You have a lot of tattoos.

Freez: A couple, yeah.

FJ: Do any of those tattoos belong to any of... No?

Freez: Before you even ask.

FJ: You've never had a girl's name tattooed...

Freez: No ma'am.

FJ: No pictures?

Freez: No ma'am.

FJ: Would you ever do that?

Freez: My wife... or my mother... or my daughter. But we gotta be family. Not no 'about to be family' or 'talking about being family.' We got to be family. It's got to be legal in the courts, everywhere. You know what I'm sayin'? Or nah, I can't see that.

FJ: I know a lot of guys have this thing where, they like a challenge. They like the thrill of the chase. What kind of lady do you prefer? One that is hard to get, or one that, you know, just...

Freez: I mean, I don't like 'hard to get' cuz, that's a game. I don't like no easy chick cuz (laughs) I do like a challenge. But at the same time, I don't like games. I don't like game. I'm-a lay my cards on the table. It's for you to either accept or reject. You know? We go from that point once you make your decision. But I don't like an overly-aggressive girl, and I don't like a too laid-back girl either.

FJ: Somewhere in the middle.

Freez: Somebody who's, you know, maybe missing a few screws and can play both ends of the field. You know? Be the aggressor at times or be the pursued at times. So...

FJ: So... Do you have a preference? Do you like a lady that's more into ladylike, prissy-type things or would you prefer a tomboy, hood girl, road dog, ride or die, etcetera?

Freez: I prefer that she be a girly-girl, but not, you know, prissy, like too good to do or touch whatever. I don't really like that too much... Just down to earth really. A lot of the chicks that I've talked to were tomboys in their pasts. But a lot of the chicks I've talked to were, you know -- One chick got the nickname, Sidity Princess, so it really -- It varies...

FJ: That's hilarious.

Freez: Yeah. One chick was "my dawg" and another was "the brat." Not Da Brat... "the brat." That's what her mama called her. So it just depends on -- I don't know. I don't really trip off of that. Just be down to earth, a girly-girl, but not too prissy.

FJ: Do you have any deal breakers, like, things you just really can't work with?

Freez: I don't like liars. You'll be surprised what another person will put up with or deal with or accept as long as you be honest about it. I don't like liars.... That was a good question... Deal breakers?... I'm thinkin' 'bout after two kids (laughter), it really can't happen. Don't get me wrong, I love kids. I have my whole life. I've always loved kids, but...

FJ: Three is too many?

Freez: I ain't gonna say three is too many, but three for me, to jump into, that's too many. Two is plenty. You know what I'm sayin'? So...

FJ: Okay.

Freez: And, oh yeah, not a Christian or not believing in Christ or whatever. That's a definite deal breaker right there.

FJ: Do you think i'ts better to have loved and lost then to never have loved before?

Freez: Only when you ain't in the pain of a heartbreak.

FJ: Okay...

Freez: Only when you're not in the pain of a heartbreak.

FJ: Right, right, right. That's a good answer. I like that. That's serious... So here's an -- Okay. First, have you ever cheated?

Freez: Yeah.

FJ: Would that be cause to scrap a relationship, like, a one-time cheat?

Freez: Would that be cause to scrap a relationship, a one-time cheat???

FJ: It just happened.

Freez: Shhhh. Ain't no just happened. I ain't never just accidentally had sex. You know what I'm sayin'? Falling and tripping, that just happens, but I ain't never just accidentally had--

Now dont get it twisted, you know...

FJ: Now, defining cheating, like, as long as there's no sex... You good?

Freez: Now, it's gonna be a problem (laughs). Whether you're cheating emotionally or physically, it's gonna be a problem. If theres no sex, then I'm more apt to be able to get over it, cuz, I mean, I have a vivid imagination, so I see things in my mind and that's just -- To my knowledge, I've never been cheated on. Notice I say, "to my knowledge," cuz y'all just got better game than what we do.

FJ: Y'all?

Freez: Females. Females just got better game than what males do.

FJ: Right, right, right.

Freez: That's the reason I say, "to my knowledge." Yeah, I wouldn't want to have to look at my chick and get that mental image in my mind. So sex, penetration, any type, yeah, I think that's pretty much 86-ing it for me right there.

FJ: So, are you more apt to hold a grudge, or do you have a hard time forgiving?... Not just with cheating. Just in general.

Freez: Umm, yeah. I can say that, yeah. I do have a hard time forgiving. I ain't never really admitted that until just now. Yeah. Yeah, I really do.

FJ: Is there a reason for that? I mean, forgiveness does take a lot, but...

Freez: Is there a reason for that? Umm...

FJ: Like you just prefer to stay in that place, in that hurt?

Freez: Sometimes it's just hard to come out of. I know growing up, I ain't feel like I really had that outlet I could go and talk to, until later on in life when I had somebody I could really go tell what was on my mind and stuff like that. So, I usually just dealt with stuff myself and the best way I could deal with it was, "Get me once, shame on you. Get me twice, shame on me." So, yeah. Depending on how bad it is and how deep the relationship is, too. Like, somebody -- If I just start kicking it with a chick and she lie to me, even if it's something small, then I don't even wanna get started with that whole little cycle. So let's just cut the deuces -- chunk the deuces right now. But if there's somebody that I've been with for a while, then I'm more than likely to forgive the lie, keep the relationship going or whatever. But honestly and truthfully, I'd still wonder. I don't like being suspicious of people, and once you cross a certain line that makes me suspicious of you, then, it is what it is.

FJ: Tell me about your worst date ever.

Freez: (laughs) Umm...

FJ: Gotta lighten it up.

Freez: Wow... Worst date ever. I remember clear as day. It was like back in '99, and met this chick at a club or whatever. We had kicked it a couple times already. I lived out in Katy. She lived off of 45 and Fuqua, so that's a good little drive. And they was working on I-10, so it was that much longer of a drive. I hate being in traffic or whatever, and I'm driving over there, stuck in traffic. It's pissing me off the whole time, pissing me off. I get over there. I'm in a little mood or whatever. She's asking me, "What's wrong?" I told her, "Nothing. Just leave me alone. Let me cool down for a minute. I don't like being in traffic. Let me calm down." She kept pushing it, kept pushing it, and I kept telling her, "It's nothing to do with you. Let me just have this little five minutes to chill out right now." Blah, blah, blah. So, she kept pushing it, kept pushing it and so, I was finally like, "Look. Shut up. Leave me alone for a minute." All right, so she got upset. We went to the movies. Saw *Cruel Intentions*. I hate that movie still to this day cuz of that night. But -- Yeah, saw the movie or whatever. So we're watching the movie and there's nobody hardly in the theatre (laughs). I can't even believe I'm finna put this out there like that. But it's nobody hardly in the theatre, right? So we started messing around, kissing or whatever. When I kissed her, you know, her mouth tasted -- didn't taste right. You know what I'm sayin'? So, when she tried to kiss me again, I'm like, "Nah, you know I don't like all that kissing." Lying and what not.

Freez & FJ: (Laugh)

FJ: You stupid.

Freez: So she like kissing on my neck or whatever, and then we chilled and start watching the movie. I forget what happened, but she got upset about something and bounced in the seat. And, out of nowhere, this odor just come and slap Ya Boi across the face.

FJ: Oh my.

Freez: Yeah, and I'm like, "Oooh, Lord," cuz at the movie theatre at 45 and Fuqua, Gulf Pointe, that one ain't the best movie theatre. So, I'm like "Ooh, Lord, let it be the seats in the theatre." You know what I'm sayin'? I'm like, "Please, please, please." Something -- I guess I didn't respond the way she wanted me to respond, so she did the little bounce in the seat again and the odor came back again. So I'm like, "I know good and hell well it wasn't the seats," at that point. So... It's time to go. We leave, and I wanted to just peel off and leave her there when she went to the bathroom, but you know, I tried to be a gentleman that night. And we got in the car. It wasn't even my car. It was my God-mama's car on top of that, right? So, we got in the car and I'm taking her home. And she just running off at the mouth, just talking a whole bunch of shit really. You know what I'm sayin'? And really trying to play me, when I already knew things that she didn't know I was aware of. So we're going down 45 and the windows down cuz I'm trying, you know, trying to let the air circulate. It's just, you know, we're on the freeway, at night, so ain't no traffic or nothing like that, and still, even with the windows down, I could still smell it. And she just gets to talking, talking, talking. I'm 20, 19 years old, and I'm like, "You know what? I ain't gotta deal with this shit. I ain't gotta deal with you talking shit. I don't have to deal with this funky ass odor in my mama's car." So I pulled over to the side of the road and let her out.

Freez & FJ: (Laugh)

Freez: She wasn't but like a half-mile from the crib, so it wasn't that, that bad.

FJ: Wow. It wasn't but a half-mile, according to you. (Laughs)

Wow.

Freez: It wasn't that bad.

FJ: So did she make it home?

Freez: I think so.

FJ: Right.

Freez: Nah, I mean -- We ended up working together, like two or three years down the line. So, yeah, I'm sure she made it home, but...

FJ: Did she say, "Remember that time when you put me out the car?"

Freez: Nah... I'm sure she could smell it too, so, she wouldn't want to bring that up.

FJ: Wow, wow, wow... That's amazing.... Best date ever.

Freez: Best date ever... Best date ever... That's a hard one cuz I haven't really dated that much... Is a Blockbuster night considered a date?

FJ: Really and truly, at this point and time, anything could be considered a date since don't nobody date no more. (Laughs) They just be talking... "We talking."

Freez: It'd have to have been a Blockbuster night or something. I don't know. I've never just had one particular date that just really stood out like that... Take that back. It was a movie night...

FJ: Movies again.

Freez: But we was talking shit through the whole movie. The only movie I've ever, well, one of only two movies I've -- I've ever come close to shedding a tear in.

FJ: Really? What movie was that?

Freez: (sniffs) Armageddon.

FJ: Wow.

Freez: My boy Bruce died. (fake crying)

FJ: So sensitive... Sooo sensitive.

Freez: A little bit. People don't get that about me.

FJ: Right, right, right.

Freez: I'm serious.

FJ: That's what's up. Do your ladies get that about you?

Freez: Yeah, once we've been together for a little bit.

FJ: Oh, so are you hard to get close to?

Freez: It's not hard to know stuff about me... but to actually let what you think about what I do, what I've done or what's happened to me, to let that affect me, yeah, that's hard. So, yeah. Cuz I try to live my life like an open book. I don't -- I'm not gonna say I'm ashamed of anything I've done or been through in my past. I think it's helped to make me who I am. So, I think by me hiding whatever things I got in my past, I think that makes it harder for the next person, who's dealt with the same situation, be free about it. So, yeah, I can tell you, like, whatever about my past and not really care how you think about it. So, you know, you're really not that close to me. You know, it's certain people who I do actually care about what they think about me and how they feel about me and so, yeah it is kinda (hard) to get to that level.

FJ: Okay. How long does it take for someone to move from just interested to girlfriend?

Freez: Unfortunately for me, most of the time, it hasn't really taken all that long if that's gonna be the move.

FJ: So like, after four dates, y'all together?

Freez: I wouldn't say that, but I know where my heart is headed at pretty soon. I say unfortunately because I've -- You know, you got that first little time period when you meet somebody and it's all lovey-dovey and whatnot. Then you decide to get together during that period. And then, you get the compatibility, the comfortability and then you can't stand each other. Yeah for me, it hasn't really taken all that long. I'd say maybe, maybe two months or so is the longest it's taken me if the girlfriend route is the way I decide to go, the relationship route or whatever.

FJ: Do you feel like, once a relationship is over, you're able to bounce back pretty easily?... Since you hold grudges and whatnot. Like, do you carry that over into your next relationship?

Freez: I don't carry it over into my next relationship. I'm not going to say it's easy to bounce back, but I don't carry it over into my next relationship. Cuz -- I won't get into another relationship if I know I'm still not really over this chick or this situation or whatever the case. I'm-a hold that off cuz I don't want to make her, the next chick, responsible for the last chick's actions, just like I don't wanna be responsible for the last dude's actions. So -- But I wouldn't say its easy to bounce back from, especially when you really care about somebody. But I don't carry it over from the next to the next.

FJ: I had a follow up question to that, but I forgot what it was. That's how it works. We're winging it... Ok, when you're in a relationship with someone, when you're in that love stage, or even before then, are you big about anniversaries, holidays, birthdays, etcetera?

Freez: No.

FJ: You don't care about those?

Freez: I mean, I make something happen because most females care about that type of stuff. But if it was up to me, nah.

FJ: So, like, let's say it's February 13th, you wouldn't remember like, "Oh, tomorrow is probably a big deal?"

Freez: Nah, I would remember it and I would make plans or whatever. But like I said, for me -- I'm not doing it for me. Well, I'm doing it for me on the back end, so I don't have to deal with the rage for not doing it.

FJ: So, do you consider yourself romantic at all?

Freez: Very much so.

FJ: Very much so?

Freez: Yeah, I think so. I just don't believe that dates, you know...

FJ: I'm not talking about dates.

Freez: I'm talking dates like anniversary dates, Sweetie's Day, Valentine's Day, those type of things.

FJ: Birthdays...

Freez: Yeah. I think a lot of relationships mess up because they wait on those days to do certain things instead of just making it a regular part of the relationship.

FJ: What was my follow-up question?... You know, don't worry about it. In your adult life or in your younger days, what was the dumbest thing you ever did for a girl, girlfriend, fiancee', etcetera, in your efforts to show your care?

Freez: The dumbest thing I've ever done in my efforts to show I care... It's actually in the book. It was with my first love or whatever. We had broken up a while back. We had been talking about getting back together and then I had my accident or whatnot. I was depressed for a long time, and she was a ride or die type of chick, you know? Real loyal, real loyal type of chick. And, I mean -- I know what I was trying to do with my life. I wasn't trying to do nothing with my life. I was trying to die. You know what I'm sayin'? It was just during that dark period in my life, I was trying to get God to see that I was ready to come home, but I wasn't going to commit suicide or nothing. So, I had committed myself to doing, you know, several things, selling drugs, being promiscuous, stuff like that. And, I mean, I felt like, to a degree, that she would stick with me through all of that, regardless. And like I say, I really care for the girl and I figured the only way to get her to see that it was time for her to move on and go about her own thing was act like I was trying to get with her best friend, and that's what I did.

FJ: So you were trying to get rid of her?

Freez: I ain't gonna say "get rid of her," cuz you get rid of something you don't want no more. But, I didn't wanna drag her through what I saw I was going to be taking myself through. I don't know. I just didn't feel at the time -- I didn't feel like I could have that talk with her to where it would've just been, "Look, you really need to go your way," or whatever.

FJ: So, do you have a hard time breaking up?

Freez: The only time I've had a hard time breaking up is with two girls who broke up with me, so I guess so. But if I'm doing the breaking up, then hey, I'm good.

FJ: Well, I mean, you said, the last one that we were just talking about, you said that you couldn't tell her, "Hey, this is the situation. I think we should go our separate ways." Obviously, that talk was hard to have, so you chose another route.

Freez: I would say with her that talk was hard to have.

FJ: So like, in general, you don't have a problem saying that, "I don't wanna be with you anymore," or, "This is not working?"

Freez: Nah.

FJ: Do you find it hard to be in a relationship when you have fans or a lot of people that know you?

Freez: I mean, it causes its difficulties. Cuz it causes suspicion and, "Oh, I know her from the poetry spot," is only gonna fly so many times, regardless to how honest you're being about the situation. Like I said, I've cheated before. I don't cheat no more. I've seen the hurt that it's caused. I know what it -- I ain't gonna say I know what it's like to be cheated on, but I know what it feels like to think you've been cheated on. I've been there. Like I say, nobody's ever actually admitted that they cheated on me. I got one or two in mind that I think, "possible." But, yeah, it can make it -- make it kind of difficult. It can get in the way.

FJ: Have you ever had any stalkers?

Freez: (Laughs) I wouldn't say stalkers.

FJ: People who couldn't let go?

Freez: I would say, yeah, a couple of those.

FJ: Were there any signs beforehand that they would be someone like that?

Freez: I mean, just the fact that it seemed like she was way into me too soon. Other than that, everything else was like, "I can't believe she doing this." The fact that she was way into me too soon would probably be the biggest sign... But I got a thing for falling fast too, so -- But at the same time I dont think I would like, stalk her.

FJ: Be standing outside the window...

Freez: You know what I'm sayin'? With an acoustic guitar and can't even play it...

FJ: Doing a driveby? (laughs)... Do you consider yourself jealous or do you have a jealous streak?

Freez: Nah, I wouldn't consider myself jealous. One girlfriend I had, we used to go out and have contests to see who could get the most numbers. That's just an example, but...

FJ: Did you win?

Freez: A couple times. Every now and then. But I mean, it's easier for a female to get a dude's number than it is for a dude to get a female's number.

FJ: That's true.

Freez: A female, a cute female can get any dude's number she sees, pretty much. You know what I'm sayin'? So, when I did win, you better understand I was showing out!

FJ: (Laughs) Interesting... Do you have or what are your thoughts on intimacy, sexual relations? I mean, do you have to be in a committed relationship for that to happen, or is it however you're feeling that night?

Freez: I mean, really, me being a Christian, believing in Christ, I believe that sex is supposed to wait until after marriage. I can't say I've always lived that way...

FJ: Are you living that way now?

Freez: Umm... (laughs) I mean, I slip. (laughs)

FJ: Is that your goal? (laughs)

Freez: We fall down, but we get up... We fall down, but we get up.

FJ: So prior to working towards that end, was it just a physical thing for you or did you actually connect emotion with it?

Freez: Nah, it wasn't until I was older in life, like, later twenties, that I started connecting sex and emotion together. Before then it was, for most chicks, it was a conquest type of situation. See if I could or just the urge to do it, you know? That type of situation. But that wasn't until the last several years that I actually equated the two.

FJ: And what brought about that change?

Freez: I had actually gotten to a point to where, I was more interested in the climax than the actual sex, and sex started becoming boring. Just going through the motions, you know, just to get to that climax. Just going through the motions or whatever. And I've always been a fan of sex, so I didn't like the idea of it getting boring to me and I took off, took some time off and chilled away to myself. Sex is good, by itself or whatever, but I just got to the point to where it's gotta be more than the urge or just because she's fine or whatever type of situation.

FJ: Now, were you ever -- Would you consider a relationship with somebody, let's say, they have no kids, but they have a baby on the way?

Freez: (long pause) No kids, but a baby on the way...

FJ: Right. So like, they just had a situation and got caught up. They're not in a relationship, but they're feeling you.

Freez: Yeah, I don't see it.

FJ: No?

Freez: That just sounds like too much drama.

FJ: (Laughs) So you try to stay away from the drama?

Freez: Yeah... I can't -- I can't do it.

FJ: Interesting... So let's say, there was a lady that was attractive to you. She had a good personality, interesting, etcetera, etcetera, but she didn't wanna work. Would that be a turn-off to you?

Freez: But she didn't wanna work?

FJ: No.

Freez: Umm... That's a good question. It depends on where I'm at financially. If I am where I'm at right now, then yeah, that's a major problem. Because right now, I can't afford to -- I'm not even living the kind of lifestyle that I want to live, so I doubt if I can afford a female who don't wanna work, who got that kind of mindset, to afford that kind of lifestyle that she wants to live. But, if I'm financially secure, you know, and set, then I don't want my wife to work. Especially if we got kids. If we have kids, then I don't want her to work. But if we don't have kids, and I can hold it down on my own, then she can work or not work. But if we got kids, I would prefer her not work, or at least not work them first five, six, seven, ten, twelve years.

FJ: (Laughs) Really? Okay.

Freez: Yeah.

FJ: Say that again.

Freez: Huh? (Laughs)

FJ: Say that again.

Freez: (Laughs) Just them first few years, something like that. I want my child to, to get that good elementary school -- You know, at least through elementary school, I want them to have that consistency and the whole nine.

FJ: Okay... Interesting... Let's say, you met a lady that was very free with her body. Very free. And she decided, "You know what? I'm saved now." It's been six months. Like, would you hold that time before against her?

Freez: Can't turn a... (laughs) Umm... I don't know. It --It -- It really depends. It -- It really depends. I mean, I'd have to -- I'm just meeting this chick or did I know her reputation from them days?

FJ: I mean, at some point the reputation is gonna come out.

Freez: Yeah, the reputation is gonna come out, but is it like, did I know her while she was living the lifestyle of that reputation, the lifestyle...?

FJ: No.

Freez: So I met her during her saved moment, period, so far..?

FJ: Yes, yeah.

Freez: Now she's on a -- I mean...

FJ: Would that change how you saw her?

Freez: Yeah, it would, just to be honest. But, if I'm already -- it depends. If I'm already feeling her, then, all right, we go from where I met you, forward. How you treat me. How you deal with me. How you deal with your life with me. You know? We could go from that. That's all I'm asking from anybody else. You know. I got skeletons in my closet. I ain't been the most faithful dude, the most honest dude. You know? We all got skeletons in our closet. But umm... Wow... umm... Yeah, that's a difficult one. It really just depends on how much I'm feeling her. It's a possibility. I wouldn't, you know, automatically rule it out, but I'm-a be checking, you know, watching the situation... That type of information, new found information, would have my antenna out a little bit more, for sure.

FJ: You say you've cheated before. Is this on multiple occasions or you had a moment?

Freez: I had a moment.

FJ: What was that moment? What made you cheat or what made you think it was a good idea?

Freez: I ain't really think it was a good idea, I wouldn't say that. But, I was in a long distance relationship. I was young, selfish, not bold enough to break off the long distance relationship prior to getting involved in what I got involved in. Pretty much, that's about it.

FJ: So, do you think there would be the possibility that you would cheat again?

Freez: I mean, the possibility?... Definitely. The possibility exists for anybody to cheat, I believe anyway. I mean, we're only human. The possibility exists. The lilkelihood of it happening, for me, is -- it's down there. It's low single digit percentages. Probably decimals or something like that. I mean, I just -- I don't know. It's certain things I don't wanna have to do. It's certain things I don't wanna have to confess to doing. And having to have that "I cheated" talk is among those things that I don't wanna have to do or have to confess to doing ever again.

FJ: So what if there was a possibility that you wouldn't have to have that talk?

Freez: I would. I would have to have that talk. I got a conscience. I've accepted it. I hated it growing up. Like, when I did cheat, I didn't have to say nothing. It was Houston and Orlando. The one that was in Houston had never been to Orlando. The one that was in Orlando had never been to Houston. They were never going to meet, you know? It was never going to come out, but you know, I got a conscience.

FJ: In general, as far as males are concerned, what do you think is the biggest reason y'all cheat?... Not special circumstances.

Freez: Biggest reason... Biggest reason men cheat. Sluts... Pretty much... You can find out what's behind the sluttery, but, yeah. It may be insecurity. It may be, you know, chauvenism. It may be whatever the case, but it boils down to sluts.

FJ: Okay... Interesting. Have you ever hit a woman?

Freez: Yep. Unfortunately. Yep. It wasn't like I just beat the chick and I don't condone it in any way, shape, form or fashion. I was in a situation with this chick for a few years and she's one of those smacking and punching and hitting types. And after a while it was like, "Hey go on with that. Go on with that," to "All right, when I hit you back, don't say nothing. All right, when I hit you back, don't say nothing." So, it kept going and I hit her in her leg a couple times.

FJ: There wasn't a point at which you thought maybe I should just get rid of her?

Freez: Yeah.

FJ: Like, forget hitting her back.

Freez: Once that happened, like, once I actually laid my hands on her, I seen it could easily escalate from that point to something way worse... Nah, it was time to go. I don't wanna be known as no Chris Brown or nothing like that. (laughs) I love ya, Chris. Keep on doing your thing.

FJ: You don't think one day, you could get real angry and somebody just push your buttons and you decide, "Let me just choke you 'til you pass out?"

Freez: Nah, cuz I'm usually gone by that time. I'm-a make my way out the door or out the situation as best I can. I mean, yeah, we're human. Everybody got their limits in everything. You can only do so much to any person before they, you know, snap. So, I think anything is a possibility. I'm not gonna say that, but -- I mean, yeah, I think it's a possibility. Like, I wasn't raised like the way a lot of dudes was raised, like, "Don't hit no females." My moms was like, "Don't let no female whup your behind neither." So, I mean, most situations, like, somebody little-bitty like you, I feel like I'd be able to handle you without having to hit you. You know what I'm sayin'. Or nothing like that. I feel like I'd be able to protect myself and defend myself without having to do you any harm. But if she a big girl (laughs) or she just, you know, that skilled with it or something, I've gotta protect myself.

FJ: Right.

Freez: I mean, I wouldn't -- That's not my forte. I don't believe in hitting no female just to, you know, to show my dominance or my strength or whatever, but if she swinging on me and I can't protect myself... (pop).

FJ: Interesting.

Freez: You know... it can happen.

FJ: Right, right, right.

Freez: I mean, it hasn't happened, but it could.

FJ: Right, right, right. Of course. In real life... That's what's up.

FJ: What is your definition of love?

Freez: My definition of love is basically, it's the continual -- I'm-a give you the Webster's, Freez break-it-down definition. It's the continual act of choosing to act and acting in the best interest of said object of love without any concern for self.

FJ: Now, you say that you have been in love three times?... Approximately?

Freez: Yeah.

FJ: Two not for real... one for real?

Freez: I wouldn't even say the other ones wasn't for real. They was love for what I knew love to be at the time. You know what I'm sayin'? What I knew love to be at the time. But looking back on it, it wasn't -- it was three different types of being in love or whatever. Three different levels.

FJ: Can you expound on those three different levels?

Freez: The first one it was like, I didn't really know what love is. I didn't even really have an idea in my mind other than it was just a feeling of really liking somebody. That's what that was. That was the first one... The second one, it was, like I say -- It was more about, I really like this chick. Really, really cut for her. I have some really strong feelings for her and the whole nine. Showed it and everything, but at the same time, you know, in the end, it was more about me.

FJ: So you loved them based on the way they loved you.

Freez: No, I was more about me.

FJ: So, the more they did for you, the more easy it was for you to be like, "Well..."

Freez: Umm...

FJ: I think that's what that is.

Freez: Nah, cuz...

FJ: There were actual true feelings...

Freez: I can't even say that they -- that the more they did for me. Cuz it wasn't the stuff that they did that made me love them. It was how they were. You know what I'm sayin'? And it was just who they were. That's why I loved them in the first place, period. I ain't gonna say, "like I did," cuz it really wasn't shown. Like I say, the first one, it was more of just a feeling. 'I really like her.' I didn't really act on that feeling, you know, as far as like, cherishing her, honoring her, stuff like that... The second one, it was -- it was more about me. My focus wasnt on her or on us. I was focused on -- on me. And on the third one, I was more focused on the health of the relationship than on me getting my way or on whether or not she's getting her way.

FJ: So do you think that love has a lot to do with compromise?

Freez: Fa sho. Definitely... You can't be in any type of loving relationship where there's no compromise. Not a mutually loving relationship.

FJ: So now that you've got your Webster's definition of love...

Freez: Freezster's.

FJ: ... and you've been through three stages of love, do you feel like you're better equipped to love someone else now?

Freez: Yeah... Yeah... Cuz now I feel like I know now that it's not just about me. You know? It's a relationship. My bad days, I want her to be understanding of my bad days so I'm-a be understanding of her bad days. Things that don't matter to me as much may matter to her that much more. You know, stuff like that, so I'm not as inconsiderate these days as I was in my younger days.

FJ: Of the three that were in the love stage, or that made it to the love stage, was there something particular that they each had that was the same?

Freez: Spoiled.

FJ: They were all spoiled?

Freez: Yeah, pretty much every chick that I've ever considered myself having been in love with or had, you know, some strong feelings for, spoiled as -- spoiled as the day is long. I don't know why. I don't get it. I don't really find being spoiled too much attractive, but...

FJ: (Laughs) Obviously you do.

Freez: (Laughs) Obviously I do.

FJ: You're gravitated.

Freez: You know, you could go name by name; Spoiled, spoiled, spoiled, spoiled, spoiled. That's the only one thing, you know, I could find in common, as far as personality wise.

FJ: So do you think that -- You say that you don't really like spoiled or whatever. Is it that they demand something from you that, let's say, some other person that's not spoiled wouldn't do, or they expect something from you so you meet that expectation?

Freez: Yeah... Yeah. I think -- I think that they, you know, definitely do demand more or expect more of me. I don't think being spoiled, per se, is a problem. You could be too spoiled, then that's a problem. But I don't think being spoiled is really a problem. I think that's why I'm attracted to 'em is because its a challenge. I know I gotta, you know -- She ain't just gonna accept any old thing. You know what I'm sayin'. So, I guess that's a part of why I like it. But when your spoiled-ness becomes so much so to where it disregards me, you just want what you want, then that's a problem. But as long as it's not to that level, I think it's cute. It's attractive, whatever.

FJ: I did mean to ask you this. Do you believe in signs?

Freez: Yes.

FJ: So like...

Freez: I don't follow 'em. I don't really notice 'em, but (laughs) but I do.

FJ: So, like, do you -- This is so funny to me... So what is it? Like, leos and...

Freez: Ohhh, those kind of signs.

FJ: Those kind of signs.

Freez: No, not really.

FJ: Like you would be uncompatible with something or other?

Freez: Not really.

FJ: No... Now, the other signs. Obviously they'll lead you the right way. But as far as little pointers people leave here and there, like, you really pay attention to the things that people say and or do?

Freez: Yeah... One thing I learned recently though is to -- I'd pay attention to what she say and what she do, but as long as she treats me straight, it's gravy. You know what I'm sayin'? But as I've gotten older, I've learned that, if she could be this way and that way to somebody that she's just met since she's known you or to somebody that's been around a lot longer than what you've been around, more than likely, she could be that same way to you. Just wait for the situation to get right. So, yeah, I've paid a lot more attention to that as I've gotten older.

FJ: Do you find that its harder to have a relationship with a female that has "daddy issues?"

Freez: Mmm hmmm, yeah, unh-hunh, yeah.

FJ: Does it cause problems in the relationship?

Freez: Yep, mmm hmmm, yeah.

FJ: (Laughs) Okay... Are they always the same problems?

Freez: I wouldn't say always the same problems, but they're very similar.

FJ: For example.

Freez: They're very similar. Some women with daddy issues, you know, daddy wasn't there or whatever, you can't really tell them nothing. "You ain't my daddy." You can't really tell her nothing. Other ones, you pretty much gotta tell 'em. You know, once they get in a relationship, it's like then they become a little girl again. You gotta take control of the relationship like a father would take control of the household and then that messes up the dynamic of the relationship or whatever. Umm... Some girls expect you to be just like their daddy. Like you know, "He left me. You gonna do the same thing," or whatever, and really haven't gotten past that. It's -- Yeah, definitely.

FJ: Difficult to deal with?

Freez: Mmm hmmm.

FJ: So do you believe the saying that how a man treats his mama is how he's gonna treat his wife?

Freez: How a man treats his mama is how he gonna treat his wife... I don't know... I don't know... Cuz -- I don't know... That's a good one. Because -- Like, my mama can still tell me what to do. I may grumble under my breath a lil bit, but you know, if she tells me to do something, nine times out of ten, I'm gonna do it. But, as far as, like, my wife or my girlfriend forcefully telling me to do something...

FJ: No, I mean like, for example, if a man has a bad relationship with his mother or he thinks low of his mother, do you think that he would have difficulty having a full fledged relationship with a woman?

Freez: Nah... Growing up, my mother and I weren't as close as a lot of other mother-son relationships. But -- I felt like, growing up, I couldn't really talk to my mom. So, that's one of the things that sparked me in writing. Because, okay, I can't talk to you, so I'm-a put it all down on paper. That way you can't interrupt me. I can get everything out the way I wanna get it out. But, I mean, for the most part in my relationships with females, I've never had a problem, you know, for the most part, expressing myself, expressing what I wanted, expressing how I felt.

FJ: Okay... Well, thats it.

Thank You's

GOD

El Dawg
Frosty
Mac
Rae
Buckethead

Layla Black
O.N.E
Deep Blu See
DJ II Deep
Dasha Flournoy
Seth Walker
Onney, "Houston's Own Poetic Diva"
Punkin' from Pluto
Seven the Poet
Franchell Jones

GOD

Coming Soon

Dear Love... Love Freez the cd

For booking, appearances, and other merchandise
please contact:

Antoine Gray
Freez 4 Life Entertainment
4422 Falcon Meadow Dr
Katy, Texas 77449
Freez4Life@gmail.com
(281) 779-0217

Follow me at:

www.WorldsColdest.com (coming soon)
www.Twitter.com/WorldsColdest
www.Facebook.com/WorldsColdest
www.Facebook.com/IAmTheWorldsColdest

Thank you for your continued support!

About the Author...

Freez Eternal, the youngest of six brothers and sisters, was born in Phoenix, Arizona in the late 1970's. At the age of six, he and most of his immediate family moved to Houston, Texas, following his parents' divorce. After graduating from high school, Freez went on to become one of, if not, the youngest ever to complete the Naval Nuclear Power Program. Upon honorable discharge, Freez spent a short time at Morehouse College in Atlanta, Georgia, but had to drop out prematurely due to financial difficulties, upon which time he chose to pursue a career in boxing. One night, while intoxicated. Freez fell asleep at the wheel of his car and faced the amputation of both of his legs as the result of the subsequent accident. With the premature end of his boxing career, Freez attended the College of Biblical Studies, where financial difficulties again proved to be unavoidable. After working in corporate America, Freez, by the urging of friends and family, chose to become, and currently is, a full time poet/spoken word artist... and now, author!

Ambit Energy
Power your future

www.ingramcontent.com/pod-product-compliance
Lightning Source LLC
LaVergne TN
LVHW020648100826
845148LV00012B/2386